Keeping Unusual Pets

Hermit Crabs

Tristan Boyer Binns

Heinemann
LIBRARY

Chicago, Illinois

www.heinemannraintree.com
Visit our website to find out more information about Heinemann-Raintree books.

To order:

☎ Phone 888-454-2279

▣ Visit www.heinemannraintree.com to browse our catalog and order online.

First published in 2004
Second edition first published in 2010

Edited by Louise Galpine, Megan Cotugno, and Laura Knowles
Designed by Kim Miracle and Ryan Frieson
Picture research by Mica Brancic
Originated by Capstone Global Library Ltd 2010
Printed and bound in China by Leo Paper Products Ltd

ISBN: 978 1 432938 54 3 (hardback)
14 13 12 11 10
10 9 8 7 6 5 4 3 2 1

Library of Congress Cataloging-in-Publication Data
Binns, Tristan Boyer, 1968-.
  Hermit crabs / Tristan Boyer Binns. -- 2nd ed.
    p. cm. -- (Keeping unusual pets)
  Includes bibliographical references and index.
  ISBN 978-1-4329-3854-3 (hc)
  1. Hermit crabs as pets--Juvenile literature. I. Title.
  SF459.H47B56 2010
  639'.67--dc22
                    2009035761

Acknowledgments
The author and publishers are grateful to the following for permission to reproduce copyright material:

Bradleyireland.com p. **11 top**; © Capstone Global Library Ltd pp. **5 top, 12, 13 top, 17, 18 top, 18 bottom, 20 top, 22 top, 22 bottom, 23 bottom, 24 bottom, 25, 26, 27 top, 27 middle, 27 bottom, 28 bottom, 29, 39 bottom, 44** (Robert Lifson), **41** (Maria Joannou), **45** (Greg Williams), **42 top, 43**; © Capstone Publishers pp. **4, 15 bottom, 16 top, 16 bottom, 19, 21, 28 top, 34 top, 34 middle, 34 bottom, 40, 42 bottom**, (Karon Dubke); C. B. & D. W. Frith p. **8 top**; Christa Wilkin pp. **5 bottom, 14, 30, 36**; Corbis pp. **35** (Jonathan Blair), **9, 24 top**; David Liebman pp. **10, 33, 38**; Getty Images p. **13 bottom** (Taxi/Georgette Douwma); iStock pp. **6** (© Jose Gil), **7** (© Igor Byrko), **20 bottom**; Kazunair Kawashima p. **8 bottom**; OSF p. **39 top** (www.photolibrary.com); Photographers Direct pp. **15 top** (Joe Bellanton), **23 top** (Gloria-Leigh Logan); Sally McCrae Kuyper pp. **32 top, 32 bottom**; Visuals Unlimited, Inc. pp. **11 bottom** (Christine L. Case), **37** (Randy Collyer).

Cover photograph of a hermit crab reproduced with permission of Alamy (© Vstock/Vstock AW).

We would like to thank Judy Tuma and Rob Lee for their invaluable help in the preparation of this book.

Every effort has been made to contact copyright holders of any material reproduced in this book. Any omissions will be rectified in subsequent printings if notice is given to the publisher.

Contents

Any words appearing in the text in bold, **like this**, are explained in the glossary.

What Is a Hermit Crab?

Hermit crabs are **crustaceans**, like all crabs. Lobsters, shrimp, and barnacles are also crustaceans. This means they have a body made of segments. They have a set of claws and four sets of legs. Hermit crabs have a hard outer skin called an **exoskeleton** that they shed when it gets too small.

Hermit crabs have two pairs of **antennae** to help them sense their surroundings. They also have eyes on the ends of stalks. They use their big, strong claws to help hold food and climb. Hermit crabs can climb trees, but they often lose their grip and fall off. Their four pairs of legs help them walk.

A hermit crab stays inside a shell almost all the time, to protect its soft body.

STAYING SAFE

Hermit crabs have soft **abdomens** that must be protected, so they live in the shells of other creatures. The shell's outer edge must not be chipped, and the inner walls should be smooth and curved. Hermit crabs are very choosy! They will not pick a damaged shell, such as one with holes that might let in sand.

Without shells, hermit crabs' soft bodies would be exposed to predators. Their main predators are birds, mammals, and larger crabs. Humans can also accidentally collect shells that are inhabited, or not empty. The stress this causes to the hermit crabs nearly always kills them.

Hermit crabs can make great pets.

Most hermit crabs wait until dark to explore, eat, and drink. They often move all their things around and tip over their water dishes!

Hermit crabs in the wild

Wild hermit crabs live in tropical areas with high temperatures and **humidity**. They lay their eggs where the tides can carry the eggs into the ocean. The eggs burst open and the new hatchlings (**larvae**) develop into hermit crabs. The hermit crabs then leave the sea to live on the sand.

Hermit crabs travel in groups of up to 100, called **colonies**. They are omnivores, which means they eat plants and animals. Hermit crabs tend to hide in their shells during the day. They are more active at night. In their natural **habitats**, hermit crabs may live for 20 years or more.

NEED TO KNOW

You should never take a hermit crab from the wild. Most countries have laws that say pets should be treated with respect. It is your responsibility to make sure your hermit crabs are healthy and well cared for.

5

Hermit Crab Facts

There are almost 500 different species of hermit crab. Most hermit crabs are **aquatic**, which means they mainly live in water. Many aquatic hermit crabs live in saltwater areas, such as sandy beaches, rocky cliffs, or wetlands. These **habitats** are exposed to the air during part of the day and submerged in saltwater for the remainder of the day.

The deep sea bottom is home to other species of hermit crabs. There are also **terrestrial** hermit crabs. That means they live primarily on land. Because these hermit crabs live in very warm climates they are most active at night.

Some land crabs will even live in trees.

What hermit crabs need

Hermit crabs need a **humid** place to live, similar to their **native** tropics. They need a layer of sand deep enough for them to bury themselves in. They need different kinds of food and clean water. Hermit crabs do not like to live alone, so plan on having at least a few hermit crabs together.

Ecuadorian crabs live near the sea.

DID YOU KNOW?

- ✪ Hermit crabs can be smaller than a penny or bigger than a softball. Generally, the bigger they are, the older they are.

- ✪ Because hermit crabs do things in groups, they make noise when their shells bang together.

- ✪ Hermit crabs come in many colors. Their color can change depending on what they eat.

Hermit crab babies

Hermit crabs come from eggs. When it is time to breed, land hermit crabs go from their inland homes to the seashore. A male hermit crab will knock on a female's shell when it is time to mate. They both come far out of their shells to mate and go back in their shells afterward. Hermit crab females then lay between 800 and 50,000 eggs. They attach the dark red-brown eggs to their **abdomens** inside their shells. While the eggs get ready to hatch, the female keeps them clean with her legs. The eggs' color changes to light blue. When the eggs are ready to hatch, the female releases them on rocks near seawater. Waves wash them into the sea.

This hermit crab is carrying her eggs until they are ready to hatch.

This photograph shows the eggs going into the seawater. They are so light; they are nearly blue in color.

As soon as the eggs hit the saltwater, they burst open and the young crabs swim out. At this point, they are called **larvae**. They look like tiny shrimp. Over the next couple of months, the larvae **molt** up to six times. They shed their old **exoskeleton** and grow a new, bigger one. They start to look like adult hermit crabs. Soon they find their first shells. Then they walk out of the sea and live on land.

DID YOU KNOW?

- ✪ Pet hermit crabs do not usually breed. A few experienced owners and scientists can raise hermit crabs from eggs.

- ✪ All the hermit crabs sold in the United States are caught in the wild and brought to pet stores.

This photograph of a hermit crab larva has been enlarged many times. The young crabs are only a few millimeters long. When they become adults, the females will return to the sea to release their eggs.

Keeping moisture in

Hermit crabs spend most of their lives making sure they do not dry out. When they are moving or eating, the parts that come out of the shell are covered in exoskeleton to keep **moisture** in. They store some water inside the shell to keep their soft abdomens moist.

Even in places that are warm and **humid**, it is too risky for hermit crabs to come out during the day to face the sunlight. They retreat all the way into their shells and close off the openings with their big claws and legs. This is one of the reasons hermit crabs change shells as they grow. A perfect fit means that even less moisture can get out.

These hermit crabs are tucking themselves away inside their shells.

Molting

Molting is when a hermit crab sheds its old exoskeleton to grow bigger. It is a time when the crab could dry out. It is careful to bury itself in moist ground or hide inside a big shell. The crab stores water inside its shell. When it comes out of the old exoskeleton, its body is soft. The water and air inside the shell helps the crab grow bigger. Then the new exoskeleton slowly hardens to protect the crab again. The hermit crab eats its old exoskeleton, probably because it is full of **minerals** such as **calcium** that help the crab form its new exoskeleton. The whole process takes about a month. Most hermit crabs molt every 12 to 18 months.

DID YOU KNOW?

You cannot force a hermit crab to come out of its shell. It will cling onto its shell.

A perfect shape

Most hermit crabs find their first shells about three months after hatching. Their abdomens will grow to fit the spiral shells. If a hermit crab cannot find the right kind of shell, its abdomen will grow to fit whatever it moves into.

This hermit crab is beginning to bury itself into the moist sand before it begins to molt.

Most hermit crabs curl like this one. They like shells with a perfect spiral because they are the most comfortable.

Is a Hermit Crab for You?

People who keep hermit crabs as pets will tell you how fascinating they are to watch and live with. They also talk about how friendly most hermit crabs are. Each has its own personality, which makes them fun to get to know.

All pets have their good points and not-so-good points. Before you decide to buy some hermit crabs, you should learn about them.

Are you ready to do all these things listed below, even when you are in a hurry or want to do something else? If the answer is yes, then you can think about getting hermit crabs!

YES OR NO?

Having hermit crabs means:

- ✪ feeding them every day
- ✪ checking that they are healthy every day
- ✪ giving them clean water every day
- ✪ bathing them weekly
- ✪ cleaning their home and toys
- ✪ giving them new shells when they are ready to move.

Hermit crabs like to drink water, and play in it! You have to make sure they always have clean water.

GOOD POINTS

⭐ Hermit crabs are interesting to watch.

⭐ Hermit crabs are not expensive to buy or feed.

⭐ Hermit crabs are quiet pets.

⭐ Hermit crabs usually stay healthy.

⭐ Hermit crabs do not take up much space.

⭐ If they are happy and well cared for, hermit crabs can live a long time. Most live 6 to 15 years, but some live 30 years as pets.

Your hermit crabs will get to know you, and you will learn all about them, too. Each one is different.

Because hermit crabs are **scavengers** in the wild, they are used to eating a wide range of food.

NOT-SO-GOOD POINTS

⭐ Hermit crabs enjoy living in groups, so you will need to have more than one.

⭐ Hermit crabs need carefully controlled homes, with the right temperature and right amount of humidity. This means you will need some special equipment.

⭐ Hermit crabs can pinch with their claws if frightened or threatened.

⭐ Sometimes hermit crabs will fight with one another.

Choosing Your Hermit Crab

Before you go to the pet store to choose your hermit crabs, you should think about what kind you want to have. Because hermit crabs are happiest in groups, you should plan to buy a few at the same time. It is a good idea to bring along an experienced hermit crab keeper to help you choose. You should never take a wild hermit crab home with you.

What size?

Hermit crabs come in different sizes. You should choose crabs close to each other in size. Most pet stores sell medium-sized hermit crabs. They are good to start with, because they are inexpensive and easy to keep happy.

What kind?

Most of the hermit crabs sold in pet stores are land hermit crabs. Land hermit crabs are also called purple pincher crabs, purple claw crabs, tree crabs, soldier crabs, and Caribbean crabs. They are less fussy about their homes, **molt** more easily, and grow larger than Ecuadorian hermit crabs. Ecuadorian crabs need saltwater to drink. They do not grow very large. But they are said to be more active, better climbers, and less likely to pinch than land hermit crabs, and they chirp. If you choose Ecuadorian hermit crabs, make sure you get two. They like to have the company of other Ecuadorian crabs.

Keeping a mixed-size group of hermit crabs takes experience. Sometimes big hermit crabs will eat smaller ones, especially when they have just molted.

WHAT TO LOOK FOR

Because hermit crabs are **nocturnal**, it is hard to see how happy and active the hermit crabs are in a pet store during the hours that the store is open! But a healthy hermit crab:

✪ might come out of its shell when you carefully pick it up and place it on your palm;

✪ should move inside its shell;

✪ should fit its shell comfortably; only the claws and two pairs of walking legs should come out;

✪ should have a clean **exoskeleton** with no scars or holes;

✪ should not have any **mites** or other bugs living on or near it;

✪ should live in a clean home with good **humidity** and no bad smells.

Hermit crabs need carefully controlled humidity. Crabs kept in a wire cage will probably be too dry.

Only choose crabs kept with the right amount of **moisture**. They will probably be less stressed out and will adapt faster to their new home.

What Do I Need?

The most important thing your hermit crabs need is a good home. It is not just a tank, but a whole **habitat**. Some hermit crab owners call their homes "crabitats." This crabitat is made up of a tank, heating, **substrate**, toys, water and food dishes. A good crabitat will keep your hermit crabs healthy for a long time.

The right tank

Because hermit crabs need high **humidity** and are good climbers, the best tank is a glass aquarium with a tightly fitting lid. A 40-liter (10-gallon) aquarium will hold about three to five hermit crabs. The glass sides and lid will keep **moisture** in and germs or chemicals out.

This crabitat is ideal. The hermit crab group is not crowded and the temperature and humidity are perfect.

If you cannot afford a glass aquarium, you can use plastic critter cages. These are harder to keep **humid**, so you will need to cover the holes. They are also usually too small for more than two crabs to live in. However, they do make good hospitals for sick or **molting** hermit crabs.

The close fit of this heavy lid means the hermit crabs will not be able to escape, and it is solid, so moisture is kept in.

What not to choose

You should not use a wire cage. Because of all the holes between the wire mesh, it is impossible to keep the proper **humidity** unless you live somewhere tropical.

This heating pad goes under the bottom of the glass aquarium, on the outside.

Heating the home

Hermit crabs need a temperature of 70° Fahrenheit (21° Celsius) to 80° Fahrenheit (27° Celsius). If they are colder, they will slow down to save energy. The best way to keep the temperature warm and even in the crabitat is to use a heating pad under the tank. Many heating pads have different settings and timers so you can get the heat just right for your hermit crabs. Some can be used with plastic critter cages as well. A heat bulb can also be used, but it will dry the air out. Hot rocks meant for reptiles do not work for hermit crabs.

Where should it go?

Because you want to be able to watch your pets easily, put their home on a table or dresser. Make sure it is not close to a window, radiator, or vent. Drafts, extreme heat or cold, and direct sunlight could kill your hermit crabs.

GOLDFISH BOWLS

Because goldfish bowls have rounded sides and very small bases, they are not good for hermit crabs. Hermit crabs need bigger bases for heaters, substrate, and dishes. Rectangular or square tanks are best.

Substrates

Hermit crabs need something to burrow in. They like to dig so they can molt, to keep **moist** and warm, and maybe just for fun. The material they dig in is called substrate. It needs to be deep enough to completely cover your hermit crabs, so about 10 to 13 centimeters (4 to 5 inches) is good.

Calci-Sand

Gravel

Play Sand

All of these materials make good substrates.

Substrates need to be smooth, so the hermit crabs do not get scratched if it gets inside their shells. Every so often you will need to clean out the tank and wash all the substrate, so it needs to be washable. Because the crabitat is humid, the substrate should not get moldy or grow bacteria easily.

Wash and dry your substrates before putting them into your crabitat.

Sand and gravel

The best substrates are sand and gravel. Play sand, carefully washed and dried, works well. Pet stores sell special Calci-Sand, which is high in **calcium** and ideal for hermit crabs. Gravel should be small, smooth pieces. If colored, it should say "aquarium safe" on the bag, or it may bleed color onto the hermit crabs. Your hermit crabs might like to have one area of sand and one area of gravel, so they can choose which substrate they like best.

HERMIT CRABS ARE NOT REPTILES

Many reptiles such as snakes and lizards live in dry, desert climates. There are many things for sale in pet shops for these reptiles. Often hermit crabs are put in the same area as reptiles. But hermit crabs are not reptiles, and will not do well with reptile bedding. Any wood shavings, bark, or crushed nutshells will hurt hermit crabs.

TOYS

Hermit crabs love to climb and explore. You can include toys in the crabitat, such as:

- ✪ dried choya wood or driftwood (but not pine or cedar—the oils in them hurt hermit crabs);

- ✪ rocks, coral, and barnacles bought in a pet store;

- ✪ clay flower pots, half-buried to make caves;

- ✪ plastic logs with hiding spots;

- ✪ plastic plants.

Some hermit crabs move their toys around at night—so you may want to glue anything heavy to the back wall of your crabitat with aquarium sealant.

Dishes

Your crabitat needs to have dishes for drinking water, food, and saltwater, too. Hermit crabs like to walk in their water dishes to drink, wash, and refill the water in their shells. You may want to partly bury the dishes in the substrate so they do not get knocked over easily.

All of these can be used as dishes in your crabitat, depending on how many hermit crabs you have and how big they are.

Shallow seashells, or plastic or cement reptile dishes that look like rocks, are good water dishes. Hermit crabs get sick from using metal water dishes. There should be something to help your hermit crabs climb out of the dish, such as stones. Make sure your water dish is no deeper than half the height of your smallest hermit crab. If the water is too deep, small crabs could drown in it.

Another similar dish should be used for a saltwater pond. Ecuadorian crabs need to drink saltwater, and even land hermit crabs like to drink a little and wash in it. A third dish should hold your hermit crabs' food.

DID YOU KNOW?

Covering the back of the crabitat with a background paper is a good idea. Hermit crabs feel safer if their tank is not open on all sides.

Humidity is the key

Hermit crabs need about 70 percent humidity. To check the humidity of your crabitat, use a humidity gauge. The water dishes in the crabitat help keep it humid, but too much humidity can help germs and mold to grow.

This is a humidity gauge. If you are not sure how to read it, ask an adult for help.

This is a nice crabitat. The hermit crabs feel safe and have plenty to do, and it is interesting for the owner to look at.

Caring for Your Hermit Crab

Hermit crabs need fresh water every day. They can get sick from water with chemicals in it, so you need to treat their water carefully. Most tap water has a chemical called **chlorine** in it. Pet stores sell drops of **dechlorinizer**, which is also called tap water conditioner. Put the drops into a container of tap water and let it sit overnight. The drops take out the chlorine. Any other harmful chemicals leave the water as it sits out. The next day, the water is ready to go into your crabitat.

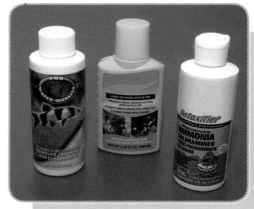

Hermit crabs drink by putting the ends of their claws into the water. They lift and pass drops of water along their legs into their mouths. They also keep a store of water inside their shells. Ecuadorian crabs keep salty water in their shells, and land hermit crabs keep fresh water in them.

These dechlorinizers will all work to take the chlorine out of your tap water and make it safe for your hermit crabs.

Bath water

For your hermit crab's bath, you will need a container that is deep enough to hold sufficient water to cover your largest crab. Tap water that has been dechlorinized and allowed to sit out overnight should be used. Occasionally, your crab can have a saltwater bath. A special salt with **minerals** that are required can be purchased at the pet store. Carefully follow the instructions on the container. Do not use table salt.

You only need a few drops to make it work.

Place your hermit crab upside down in the bath. Water will go into its shell. Watch your crab turn right side up. When it does that, the water will flush out any dirt or food that may have been caught in the shell. You can repeat this process if your pet is very dirty.

Going on vacation

Hermit crabs are tough, but they do require care. If you are going away for more than a day, you'll need to find someone to care for your pets every day by giving them clean water and food. If you are going away for a long time, you may want to find someone who can take your crabitat home. Either way, train someone who is new to hermit crabs or find an experienced owner to help you.

There should be a saltwater dish in your crabitat at all times. The saltwater needs to be changed every day.

MIXING IT UP

Hermit crabs know how much salt they need. If their saltwater is too salty, they will drink freshwater until the overall water they have drank is just right for them.

Giving your hermit crabs a bath in dechlorinized water helps to keep them healthy.

Feeding your hermit crab

In the wild, hermit crabs are **scavengers**. This means they do not hunt for their food. Instead they eat what they can find. They eat all sorts of food, from fruit and plants, to dead animals, to insects, to other animals' **feces**. They can smell food from about two meters (six feet) away, or further if it is very smelly.

Kinds of food

Your hermit crabs need two kinds of food. First they need hermit crab food made especially for them. This goes in their food bowl. It should always be there for them. **Moist** food needs to be changed every day but dry food can last a couple of days.

Hermit crabs see others eating and join them. They can end up as a very big group eating together.

Hermit crabs also need treats. Because they eat so many kinds of food in the wild, they like to eat lots of different treats as pets too. Put the treat in the crabitat for about 15 minutes, then take out anything that's left.

Hermit crabs also need extra **calcium**. It is best to give them cuttlebone, which is sold in pet stores. It can stay in the crabitat since it does not spoil.

There are many kinds of hermit crab foods. Large pieces will need to be crushed for small hermit crabs. Some dry food needs to have water added to it.

Keeping it neat

Hermit crabs can make a mess of their food. They like to take food out of the dish and move it around. They will often eat some, move some, and bury the rest. They also try to hide food. To keep your crabitat clean, you need to look for uneaten food and remove it. If it is left too long, it will start to rot and smell badly.

After dark

In the wild, hermit crabs do most of their eating after dark. To keep them happiest, you should change their food and give them treats late in the day or after dark.

TOP TIP

You do not need to worry about hermit crabs overeating. They will usually eat just the right amount. Read the instructions on the food you buy. Some food needs to have water added. If your hermit crabs do not eat much of one kind, try another kind. Maybe moist food would make them happier than dry food, or vice versa.

GOOD HERMIT CRAB TREATS

Grapes	Leafy green lettuce
Cooked rice	Dried shrimp
Plain popcorn	Mangoes
Raisins	Crackers
Oatmeal	Seaweed
Applesauce	Cooked meat
Peanut butter	Bread
Plain pasta	Brine shrimp
Fresh fish	

It is a good idea to give treats often and to try and give different foods each time.

Keeping clean

Hermit crabs clean themselves by **grooming**. They use their legs and claws to brush dirt and sand off their bodies. They also clean their shells this way. They need to keep small pieces of grit off their bodies. Anything that rubs can tear into their **exoskeletons** and hurt the thin places where they bend. Their **abdomens** can get badly hurt by rough things rubbing against them. If your hermit crabs have clean water and enough humidity, they will keep themselves clean. But most hermit crab owners like to give them baths, too.

When to clean

Hermit crabs seem to like to have baths. Most people give them baths between twice a week and every two weeks. Baths help keep hermit crabs moist and let you watch out for pests such as **mites**. Hermit crabs will drown if left in water over their shells for too long. Always watch your hermit crabs during their baths, and take them out of the water after a few minutes.

This hermit has just finished its bath and is drying off on a paper towel.

BATH TIME

What you need:

- ✪ a nonmetal container of room temperature dechlorinized water

- ✪ a container lined with several layers of paper towel.

What to do:

- ✪ Put your hermit crabs in one at a time upside down into the bathwater container.

- ✪ When the crab peeks out of the shell and kicks its legs, dirt will be washed off. It should turn itself right side up. You do not need to scrub or wipe your crabs.

- ✪ Most crabs will move a lot during a bath, so watch them carefully!

- ✪ Take the crab carefully out of the bath container and put it into the drying container. Let it walk around until it is dry. If it goes back into the crabitat wet, the **substrate** will get soggy.

Aloe Vera

Many hermit crab owners like to put some special aloe vera drops called Stress Coat into the bathwater. Aloe helps the hermit crabs' exoskeletons stay strong and smooth. It also helps keep their gills moist for breathing.

Cleaning the crabitat

To keep your hermit crab safe from mold and germs, you need to completely clean out the crabitat every one to three months. You need to take your hermit crabs out before you can clean their home. This is best done after their bath. While they are drying off in an escape-proof container, you can take all the dishes, sponges, toys, and shells out of the crabitat. Wash dishes with hot water and dry with paper towels. Sponges should be washed in hot water and then rinsed through with saltwater. They should be left to air dry. Toys should be washed in hot water. Shells, rocks, and coral can be boiled to get them really clean.

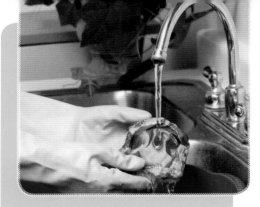

Clean dishes help to keep your pets healthy.

Ask an adult to help you clean your shells by boiling them for five minutes.

EVERY DAY

- ✪ Give new water.
- ✪ Give new food.
- ✪ Give a treat.
- ✪ Clean out any old food and droppings in the substrate.
- ✪ Check temperature and humidity.
- ✪ Check if sponge is clean— wash if needed.
- ✪ Check for any molting or sick crabs.

EVERY WEEK

- ✪ Clean the bowls and air or towel dry them.
- ✪ Clean toys and shells.
- ✪ Check if substrate is clean by sifting through it.
- ✪ Move shells around.

Substrate

Sand and gravel can be cleaned in two ways. The easiest way is to replace it completely with new substrate. The other way is to clean it and reuse it. Washing it through a strainer in hot

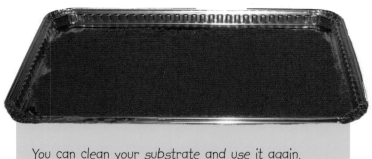

You can clean your substrate and use it again.

water is the first step. Then, spread it out on a baking sheet. Ask an adult to help you heat it in an oven at 300° Fahrenheit (149° Celsius) for 30 to 45 minutes to kill mold and germs. Let it cool down and dry completely before you put it back in the crabitat.

Finally, you need to clean the tank. Use a mixture of water and vinegar, or saltwater, and wipe the entire tank carefully. Then rinse the entire tank by wiping it with hot water. Thoroughly dry the tank. Now you can put your crabitat back together and return your pets to their home.

No chemicals allowed

Hermit crabs get sick from chemicals very easily. You must not use any cleaning chemicals such as bleach, or even soap. Even normal table salt can hurt hermit crabs, so make sure you only use products made for fish and aquariums.

Funny Smells

Your crabitat should not smell badly. If it does, try feeding your crabs less smelly treats. Also look more carefully for buried and hidden food. If you have many hermit crabs, you should look for dead hermit crabs.

Shedding Shells

All hermit crabs **molt** to grow bigger. Adults molt about once a year. As their **exoskeletons** get too small, they slow down, get cloudy eyes, eat a lot and then stop eating, and then usually bury themselves in the **substrate**. A molting hermit crab has no hard exoskeleton, so it tries to protect itself underground. Covering up keeps **moisture** in and other animals out while the new exoskeleton hardens.

Many owners look for hermit crabs about to molt and move them to separate crabitats. These are just tanks with substrate for the molting crabs to dig into. Give them food and water, and keep the substrate moister than usual. If you cannot set up a separate molting tank, you can use the top half of a plastic soda bottle to protect molting crabs. Do not bother a molting crab, try to dig it up, or give it a bath.

This hermit crab has just molted, and is tucked away in his shell. The empty exoskeleton is on the left.

Most hermit crabs bury themselves in the substrate when they begin to molt. However, some molt on the surface of the substrate. The crabitat should have enough substrate to cover the largest crab with several inches of substrate.

Some hermit crabs may take a day to molt and others may take over a month. First the old exoskeleton splits along its back. Then the hermit crab wiggles free. It waits inside its shell for its new exoskeleton to harden. It often eats the old exoskeleton. When it is ready to come out, it digs back up to the surface. It may look for a new, larger shell.

No warning

Hermit crabs do not always give clear signs that they are about to molt. You may suddenly find what looks like a dead hermit crab in the crabitat. You may pick up one of your pets and have what seems to be its body fall out of its shell. Before you worry, check that it is not an old exoskeleton. Your crab may have molted suddenly and be just fine inside its shell.

DID YOU KNOW?

Hermit crabs urinate through their **antennae**—and never enough at one time for you to see it! Hermit crab **feces** are hard and dry and do not smell.

Changing shells

Hermit crabs will change shells when they **molt** and grow bigger, but also sometimes for no reason. Every crab should have two or three extra shells available at all times. Perfect hermit crab shells have no holes in them and a smooth inside. This means the **abdomen** will stay **moist** and not be hurt by roughness or dirt.

You should buy shells from pet stores and dealers who will collect them carefully and wash them well before selling them. Before you give a new shell to your hermit crabs, ask an adult to help you boil it for five minutes.

Land hermit crabs love shells with round openings and smooth, shiny insides.

Ecuadorian crabs love shells with dull insides and oval openings.

These shells are very colorful. Only buy them from pet stores and hermit crab experts, so you know they are safe for your pets.

New hermit crab, new shells

When you bring a new hermit crab home, give it a bath to make sure it has no **mites** or dirt in its shell. Rub the outer surface of its shell with a paper towel if it is dirty. When you get a new hermit crab, get some new shells for it, too. Often a new pet will want to change shells soon after it gets used to its new home. Keep the new crab away from the rest until it seems to you to be acting normally and healthy. This takes between a day and two weeks. Then put your new crab into the crabitat and watch to make sure there are no fights. You may want to put the new crab in after all the hermit crabs have had a bath, so they all smell the same.

SIZING THE SHELL

Hermit crabs should be able to pull all the way back into their shells and cover the openings with their claw and one leg. If they do not fit, they will look for new shells. Some crabs like shells that are too small or too big. This is fine. Never try to force your hermit crabs to change shells.

Handling Your Hermit Crab

Hermit crabs are less likely to pinch than other crabs, but they still do sometimes! It is a good idea to learn how to safely hold them. Because hermit crabs have pointed legs and use their claws to help walk, it will always feel a bit prickly to hold your pet.

To pick up a hermit crab

- ✪ You may want to wear gloves until you and your crab get used to each other.
- ✪ Plan to hold it over a soft place, such as a bed or cushion, so it will not get hurt if you drop it.
- ✪ Lift it by the back of its shell onto your hand.

- ✪ Stretch out your hand.
- ✪ Let the hermit crab walk from palm to palm if it wants to.
- ✪ Hold your pet in one hand and offer it a treat with the other hand.
- ✪ Remember to be slow and gentle with your hermit crab—moving quickly could scare it and make it pinch.

Fights

Hermit crabs use their claws to fight one another for shells. The fighter will knock the victim on the shell, then try to shake it out or pull it out with its big claw. If the victim is shaken out, it will probably be fine. The fighter will move into the victim's shell, and the victim will move into the fighter's shell. But the victim may go back into its shell and defend the opening with its big claw. If the fighter pulls hard enough, it could pull the victim's claw off. This does not mean the victim will die, because hermit crabs can lose legs and claws and still live.

The legs and claws usually grow back the next time the crab **molts**. But it is good to watch out for shell fights and move the crabs apart. Make sure there are enough shells in your crabitat so shell fights will not occur. Hermit crabs also wave and knock their **antennae** together, but this is usually harmless. Climbing over each other and pushing crabs out of the way is also harmless.

Help! Ouch!

If your hermit crab pinches you and will not let go, do not try to pry it loose or shake it off. The best thing is to hold it briefly underwater and it will loosen its grip. Make sure you are holding it close to the bottom of the sink or tub, so it does not fall far when it lets go.

Shell fights can look scary. Usually they end up just fine.

Some Health Problems

Hermit crabs are generally healthy pets. You do not need to take them to the vet for check-ups or shots. What makes them sick most often is stress. Not having the right food and living conditions makes hermit crabs stressed. Making sure you have a big enough crabitat; keeping it clean, warm, and **humid**; and giving your pets enough shells will keep them healthy. But if all these things are good and your pet does something odd or changes its habits, it may be sick. Here are some of the things that can go wrong. If you are in any doubt, ask your vet or an expert for help.

Hermit crab signals

First think about when it last **molted**. If it has been a few months to a year, and the hermit crab isn't eating, isn't moving much, and its eyes have gone cloudy, maybe it is ready to molt. Digging itself under the **substrate** and staying there is another sign that it may be ready to molt.

You can place your hermit crab in the palm of your hand in order to take a closer look at it. Check to see if its eyes are cloudy. Maybe your hermit crab is getting ready to molt.

Falling apart

If your hermit crab suddenly starts to drop legs, it is probably feeling stressed. It can happen soon after you bring it home. It may have had a long trip from its home to the pet store, and it may have lived in stressful conditions. The best thing to do is to keep it quiet and dark, separated from other hermit crabs. Give it ideal living conditions. After a couple of weeks, put it into the main crabitat. Watch to make certain it has been accepted. At its next molt, the missing legs will come back.

DIFFICULT CHARACTERS

Some hermit crabs fight a lot. The fighter may be feeling stressed. Try giving it time on its own in a separate tank. It may need more shells to move into or somewhere quiet to hide. When the fighter seems calmer, put it back to the main crabitat and watch carefully. Usually it will calm down and be friendly. If yours does not, you may need to keep it on its own a little longer and then try again.

Check your crabitat if you hear a lot of chirping, because this can mean there is a shell fight or simply that one hermit crab is sitting on top of another.

Naked hermit crabs

One of your hermit crabs may suddenly be naked one morning—due to a shell fight it lost, because it was too hot, or for some other reason. If it seems otherwise well, try to get it back into its shell.

- ✪ Check the empty shell. Make sure it is smooth and unbroken all the way inside. Boil it for five minutes, then run it under cool water so it is not too hot.

- ✪ Carefully dip the naked crab in crab bathwater.

- ✪ Hold the shell, and gently place the crab back in.

- ✪ If it does not go right back in, tap its head. This will make it draw into the shell to protect itself.

- ✪ If this does not work, try a larger shell.

If a naked hermit crab does not seem well or will not go back into a shell, call your vet or ask an expert for help.

Bugs

Sometimes hermit crabs get small white bugs called **mites**. Mites may simply crawl in and decide to live in your crabitat, or they may be brought in with a new crab or toy. Here is how to get rid of mites.

- ✪ Bathe all your hermit crabs until no more mites come out of their shells. This may take four baths or more. Pour the used bath water down the drain each time to get rid of the mites.

- ✪ Leave the hermit crabs to dry in a clean place.

- ✪ Take everything out of the crabitat and clean it very well. Make sure you sterilize or replace all your **substrate** and toys.

- ✪ Wash the tank out with vinegar and rinse with water.

- ✪ Use damp paper towels to make sure all the mites are gone from the tank.

- ✪ Throw out any wood and live plants that were in the crabitat. Mites are almost impossible to get out of wood, and they love wood and plants.

After wiping all the corners and glass with damp paper towels to make sure all the mites are gone, thoroughly dry the tank.

TOP TIP

Make sure the crabitat lid fits well, you clean your crabitat often, and you do not leave treats and food to spoil. This should help you stay mite-free in the future. Wiping all the corners and glass with damp paper towels will make sure all the mites are gone.

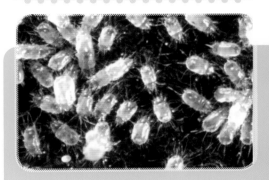

It is important to bathe new crabs and wash all crabitat items properly to keep little white mites away from your crabitat.

Fungus

Sometimes a hermit crab will grow **fungus** on its body. It looks like fluffy white cotton candy. It can be cured by giving the hermit crab a room temperature bath with twice the amount of salt you usually put in the bath water container. Gently put the crab in the bath, tilting it so that the saltwater fills the shell. Set the crab on some paper towels to dry, then place it in a rinse bath with an aloe conditioner. Remember that a hermit crab can be easily stressed. If the bath does not get rid of the fungus, check with your vet or a hermit crab expert.

HOUSEHOLD HAZARDS

If your hermit crab is very happy being out of its crabitat, you may let it out in your home for short periods of time. You need to watch carefully while it is out, because it may get hurt by:

✪ climbing up something such as a curtain and then falling off

✪ getting legs or claws stuck in carpets or fabrics

✪ falling off high places, such as tables or beds

✪ getting attacked by other pets.

When your pet is out of its crabitat, it is best to keep it on a smooth surface and to keep other animals and small children away.

Saying good-bye

Most pet hermit crabs live for about one year, and many live for 6 to 15 years. If you keep yours in an appropriate crabitat and give thm proper care, they should live a long time. Sadly, however well you care for your hermit crab, one day it will die. Sometimes a hermit crab will just die peacefully in the crabitat. This may be a shock to you, but do not blame yourself. There was probably nothing you could have done.

Sometimes a hermit crab will bury itself in the **substrate** and stay there. After a month, check that it is still alive by smoothing the sand on top and seeing if there are any signs of digging in the morning.

Sometimes a hermit crab will have had too much stress to live. It may come home from the pet store and lose all its legs and claws. It may have lost a shell fight or have been attacked by another hermit crab. If this happens, you can keep it safe, quiet, and as comfortable as possible while it either heals or dies.

Sometimes it helps to have a special burial place for your pet.

FEELING UPSET

However it happens, you will feel upset when a pet dies, especially if it has been a friend for years. It is perfectly normal for people—even adults—to cry when a pet dies or when they think of a dead pet.

Keeping a Record

It is fun to watch your hermit crabs and take notes about what they do. Keeping a record of your pets is a good idea. You can write down important dates and measurements. Buy a big scrapbook, and fill it with photos and notes.

A special diary

You could start your scrapbook the day you set up your crabitat for the first time. Write down what you use for **substrate**, toys, dishes, heaters, and anything else.

Note the temperature and **humidity**. Put in photos of what it looked like before you brought any hermit crabs home.

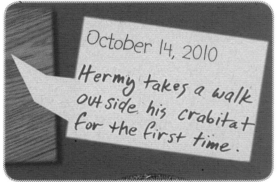

October 14, 2010

Hermy takes a walk outside his crabitat for the first time.

Next, you could write about your first hermit crabs — how you picked them out in the pet store, why you chose them, how you felt bringing them home. Take photos of them and label them with their names and the dates you got them. You could take notes about when you put them into the main crabitat, how they acted, and any funny things they did.

Ask someone to take photos of you with your pets for your scrapbook.

It is helpful to note what kinds of food and treats your hermit crabs like best. If they have any illnesses or are fighters, write down what happened and how you coped with it. The phone numbers of your vet and hermit crab experts should also be in your records. If anything goes wrong again, you can look back at your notes for help.

Whenever your pets do funny or amazing things, take photos and write down what happened. You will soon have a fascinating scrapbook of memories and references to look back at.

IMPORTANT INFORMATION

You can record a lot about every hermit crab. Keeping a page for each one is a good idea. You can update the information each time the hermit crab molts or changes shells. Here are some suggestions for the information you can include about each crab:

- ✪ Name
- ✪ Date brought home
- ✪ Width of shell opening
- ✪ Width of big claw
- ✪ Color
- ✪ Date **molted**
- ✪ Date changed shell
- ✪ Shell type
- ✪ Special likes
- ✪ Illnesses

HERMY

September 14, 2010
Hermy's first crabitat.

October 14, 2010
Hermy takes a walk outside his crabitat for the first time.

November 14, 2010
We have our first junior crabbers club meeting.

Your scrapbook is a great way to show and tell friends about your hermit crabs. You could take it to school and show your teachers, too.

Understanding Hermit Crabs

Many people keep hermit crabs as pets. Some start with a few and then find themselves the proud owners of many hermit crabs. No matter how many hermit crabs you have, you must remember that each one requires care. When you have your own hermit crabs, you will want to find out more about them as you grow to love them.

Sharing the fun

Ask at your school and at the local pet store if there are other hermit crab owners near you. There may be hermit crab clubs nearby that you could join. They will have meetings to talk about hermit crabs, share ideas, and help each other out. If there are no clubs already, you could ask an adult to help you start a hermit crab club of your own.

It is fun to talk about your pets with other hermit crab owners.

NOW FIND OUT EVEN MORE

Here are some ways to find out more about hermit crabs:

✪ Look for books at your local library.

✪ Visit aquariums.

✪ With an adult, visit some hermit crab websites. Some are set up by companies that sell hermit crab things, and some are from hermit crab groups. Others are by people who simply love their pets! Most have a lot of great pictures and useful information.

✪ With an adult's help, join a hermit crab message board or discussion group online. Hundreds of pet owners are members, posting messages about their pets. This can be a useful way to get information. However, if your pet seems sick, always consult your vet or a hermit crab expert.

✪ Check out pet magazines. There are none just for hermit crabs, but they are included in some general small or unusual pet magazines. Magazines are great sources for up-to-date information.

An adult can help you find information about hermit crabs on the Internet.

Glossary

abdomen part of a segmented animal that has most of its organs, such as the stomach

antenna long, thin feeler on the head of a hermit crab and some other animals

aquatic living in or near water

calcium kind of mineral that helps make bones and hard shells such as exoskeletons

chlorine chemical found in most tap water and swimming pool water

crustacean kind of animal with a segmented body and a hard outer shell

dechlorinizer special liquid that takes chlorine out of tap water

exoskeleton hard outer skin on an animal that does not have bones

feces solid waste matter passed out of the body (poo)

fungus kind of plant that grows on other plants or animals. Mushrooms and mold are types of fungus.

grooming cleaning an animal's body

habitat place where an animal or plant lives or grows

humid having a large amount of water in the air

humidity amount of water in the air

larva very young animal after it hatches from its egg and before it grows into an adult

mineral found in food, and helps keep animals and people healthy

mite small blood-sucking insect

moist slightly wet

moisture water that is present in the air that forms tiny drops on a surface

molt shed an old exoskeleton so the animal inside can grow bigger

native place where an animal comes from or lives in the wild

nocturnal awake and active at night

scavenger animal that feeds on what it can find instead of hunting for live food

substrate material put on the bottom of the crabitat

terrestrial living on land, rather than in water

Find out more

Books

Carle, Eric, et. al. *A House for Hermit Crab*. New York: Simon and Schuster Children's Publishing, 2009.

Pavia, Audrey. *Hermit Crab: Your Happy Healthy Pet*. Hoboken, N.J.: Howell Book House, 2006.

Stevens, Kathryn. *Hermit Crabs*. Mankato, Minn.: Child's World, 2009.

Websites

www.pethermitcrab.com
This website has lots of information on hermit crabs and how to look after them.

www.hermitcrabs.org
This hermit crab website includes information on shells, molting, temperature, and food.

Index